FIGHT TO THE FINISH

COPYRIGHT © 2020. ALL RIGHTS RESERVED.

No part of this publication may be reproduced, distributed, or transmitted in any form or by any means, including photocopying, recording, or other electronic or mechanical methods, or by any information storage and retrieval system without the prior written permission of the publisher, except in the case of very brief quotations embodied in critical reviews and certain other noncommercial uses permitted by copyright law

MEET STEVEN

Steven is a boy with a great passion for success. Steven doesn't play a lot of video games. He has a strong physical ability.

His parents believed he could do well in the sport of wrestling. They believed that wrestling will contribute to his physical and mental strength. The belief is he will grow through the sport.

He'll learn how to make important decisions for himself and grow physically.

His parents explain why he needs to wrestle. They explained to him there's age and weight categories.

Wrestling will tame his fears and worries.

He'll be conditioned through constant training and build strength. He'll have the body he wants. He'll be very balanced and coordinated. He can control someone else. Wrestling will let him use his energy well, while he's still young. His parents did let him know, he won't win every match, but he can win most with hard work. By this, he'll have a sense of greatness. It will be fun to learn, practice, and show his moves. Most importantly, he'll learn how to relate to kids.

Steven's father took him to wrestling center for registration the next day.

He very was happy, but had some fears. He was doubting if he could do it.

The coach was very happy to meet Steven. He told Steven everything he needed to know about practices and tournaments. Steven was happy and couldn't wait to start.

LIFE LESSONS FROM WRESTLING...

The first few weeks of practice, Steven was catching on fast. One evening, the coach called all the kids together.

He start telling of life lessons that come with wrestling. He said there's no greater test than you battling with another person in this sport.

The one-on-one battles will have you meet different opponents. Just know there will be someone better than you. You can be the best, but understand that the best is somewhere else also. Be humble. Don't subject yourself only to the joy of winning. You can't win every time. Be ready for defeats, and don't ever blame others.

Your success in wrestling depends on how hardworking you are. How you practice will make you standout. In life. Your success will depend on how best you prepare yourself for whatever it is you want to be.

Your attitude towards work will make you stand out. Wrestling will let you know your limits. You can be the strongest in the world. But knowing your body limitation is a great gift. This will serve you well for the rest of your life. You'll know where your strength lies and how to face challenges in life. The intense physical foundation you're building for yourself, will inform your mind on making important decisions in **life**.

When you win a match, it means you've imposed your will on your opponents. Don't bragging or talk bad about that person. When you practice at a high level you'll be confident about yourself. You'll have the confidence in yourself that you will win.

You won't win every match. That's a good thing. Learn from that lost. Then win the next match. Wrestling is a individual sport.

Your teammates and coaches won't be there to take your blame always. Your performance should be of great interest to you, during practices and competition. Learn how to support your teammates.

You should want to see your team and teammates win. Your teammates will become your friends.

By cheering them to succeed. They will also do what is necessary to help you succeed also. You'll need these kind of FREINDS in life. Wrestling will teach you how to work with people as a team. Your determination should be on what you've planned to achieve together in any work setting you find yourself. Teamwork won't be an issue. Your mental ability is more important than physical strength.

You'll learn how to guide your mind because wrestling starts from within.

Wrestling will teach you how to control your emotions before or during the match. Your mental ability is needed for success as you grow through life. Let wrestling become your lifestyle. It requires your dedication and discipline on and off the mat.

Wrestling is not for everyone. But everyone that participates will be rewarded greatly. You'll have whats needed for a good life.

A life without discipline, is like a motor without a brake. Such a motor will end in an accident. Wrestling will give you the best form of control that you require to run your race. Wrestling will make you useful in life.

When the coach was done talking, the kids where very eager to do their best. Steven also remembered what his father had told him.

The time spent in wrestling is never wasted time.

Don't fear commitment,

FEAR wasting your TIME...

Time is something you can never get back. Use it wisely...

THE COMPETITION...

Steven found out when the first tournament was. He was overjoyed but also afraid. When he got to the tournament, he'd never seen so many kids in one place. This made him more afraid. He was so afraid till he begged his parents to take him home. They let him know everything will be ok. When Steven's was called for pairing. His father had to carry him to the pairing area. Steven and the kid he was paired with got the mat they'll be wrestling on. Steven was so afraid. The kid he was going to wrestle, couldn't wait to get on the mat to wrestle.

When it came time to wrestle,

Steven was so afraid till he was pinned very fast.

The other kid was so happy to win.

His family was cheering him.

Steven cried, then was begging his parents to take him home.

Stevens coach pulled him aside. He told Steven.

Now you know you won't go undefeated.

You're going to win some and lose some, it's a part of the game. What you have to do now is get yourself together. Say to yourself, I'm going to give it my all my next match and see what happens.

You have nothing to lose, you've already lost once now go out there and use everything you learn these past few weeks in practice. You always want to say, you gave it your all no matter the outcome.

When it came time for the next match, Steven put in his mind he's going to give it his all and not give up or be afraid. When the match started Steven went out there like a monster and totally destroyed the other kid. The kid didn't know what hit him Steven's parents and coaches was so happy for him.

Steven kept that same mind the next matches and he won them all. Steven's last match was against first kid who beat him. The kid figured it would be an easy win again. To his surprise. Steven return the favor and pinned him even faster than Steven was pinned.

Now that kid was crying like a baby.

From then on Steven kept the mind to give it his all no matter what. He didn't win every match but he had a very good season.

REMEMBER: Never give up...

THE MIND OF A WRESTLER...

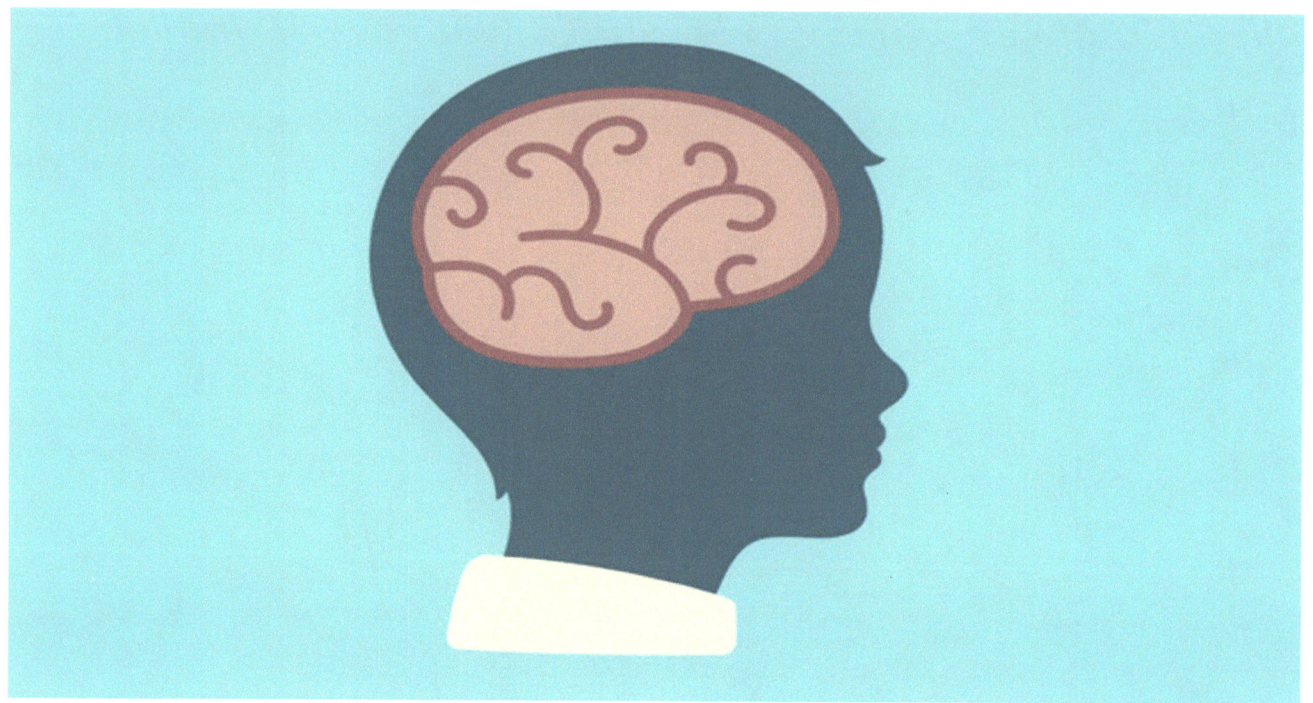

Wrestlers believe they can always do better. Always believe in yourself. You're a wrestler even though you're not on the mat. Consider the wrestling mat to be your lifes journey you have to win. The best way to overcome all challenges. Is to be grateful for every opportunity presented to you.

Always be happy whenever you're asked to prove yourself. Don't be too aggressive, but instead, be relentless. A wrestler will never give-up easily.

You'll face fears as you grow. But be like Steven who had a hard time silencing his fears. Your first victory will take place in the mind.

Guide your heart and make sure you don't give up.

The great stars of the world you see today also worked on themselves too. You wouldn't have heard their names if they had given up.

Just like Steven, many hearty cheers are waiting for you. NEVER GIVE UP...

Good Luck...